Hull
City Council

Working in partnership

AN INTRODUCTION TO
GAME
WRITING

A WORKBOOK FOR
INTERACTIVE STORIES

"This book will help a lot of people who are trying to make sensible content from the ideas in their head."

– Laura Macdonald, Game Writer

DEDICATION

To my late parents, Joyce and Bernard

Your love, support and hefty indulgence
led me to the career I enjoy today.

ACKNOWLEDGMENTS

Many thanks to Christina Longden, Laura MacDonald, Monica Graham Garcia, Shea Graham-Dolph and Stephen Brown for excellent feedback, general help and very kind words.

Thanks, too, to Stephen Dinehart for ongoing support and being a true creative.

This book couldn't exist without all of the talented people I've had the pleasure and honour of working with over the years, particularly the good people of Revolution Software. They are too numerous to mention individually but they know who they are.

Foreword

Games and story are deeply intertwined; it's often challenging to separate one from the other. It can lead to some interesting arguments about what a game is, what a story is and what it means to be a player in a story. The way to get there is often a combination of game design and game writing.

Game writing can mean many things, but in the big budget video game industry it often means the person who writes dialog. In essence, it's sort of like being a playwright where the stage is the game and your audience is an actor.

People like Steve Ince and I are storytellers, artists, engineers and writers that work very hard to make a range of elements come together like a symphony, one that you get to direct through your actions, by playing the spectacle, or an "interactive story". Sometimes that means doing just a little part on a big project, but other times that means doing everything on a little project which seems too big.

It takes a lot of care and attention regardless, curiosity for how things work and a general desire to make them better. This is really a new form of story, at least to our knowledge, where the audience gets to become part of it rather than just a passive observer. I often tell people if they are interested in their own story go write a book.

In interactive stories you get to communicate in different ways than previous authors and artists, and you have to allow room for choice and chance. For some traditional authors that's quite challenging. In recent decades there has been a lot of evolution of this form, the database narrative, but it's hardly finished, possibly even mature.

What Steve Ince presents here is a great way to start thinking about and creating your own interactive stories in any medium. I wish someone handed me this book a long time ago. Who knows, maybe one day you can invite Steve and I to come play one of your stories? We're very confident in you, just do your best.

Sincerely,

Stephen E. Dinehart IV

Spring 2021

Is this book for you?

If you've never written an interactive story in your life and would love to do so, this book is **definitely** for you!

If you love storytelling and have a million ideas flying around in your head all the time, then you should **absolutely** read this book.

If the idea of becoming a game writer is a dream you long to fulfil but have no idea where to start, reading this book will introduce you to the subject in a clear, easy-to-follow way.

Nothing in this book requires you to have any previous knowledge of game writing or development. Nor does it expect outstanding English or knowledge of literary devices.

All that's needed from you is a love of storytelling and a desire to tell your stories in an interactive way. You can be a young person or an adult, from any kind of background and with any range of interests.

This book IS for you.

For teachers, parents, school librarians, youth organisations, literacy groups, public libraries, etc. – this book will provide a fresh look at storytelling and writing, which will fire up those people you work with in a way they can directly relate to.

There are many opportunities to enhance the book by inserting lessons on spelling, grammar, sentence construction, etc. Also, you could devise your own themes and story ideas to fit in with those of other lessons. Interactive storytelling will only ever enhance these things.

Chapter 1 – About the Book

The book you're now reading is an introduction to the principles of interactive writing in general and game writing in particular. For those who have no starting point for this exciting way of writing, you will find the right kind of help you need.

You may be ten years old or a hundred, but your age doesn't matter when you set out on a journey to discover new skills. This book will work for everyone who has the urge to learn.

What's most important, regardless of age or general experience, is that you use this book with open eyes and an eagerness to learn one of the most exciting and rewarding ways to tell stories.

For those of you who know very little about games, I will show, step by step, how writing and storytelling can be applied to games.

Twine

As the book progresses, I'm going to be using Twine to show how to build your stories. The beauty of Twine is the way complete beginners find it easy to learn and use. Yet it contains a strong set of features that enable you to tell the richest of stories. It's great to share them with your friends, too.

You can either download Twine from **twinery.org** or use it directly on their website. As this is open source software, it's free to download, but if you like using it then please consider making a small donation.

Knowledge and Experience

Sharing knowledge and experience is important for all of us, so I hope this book gives you a start in your quest to become a game writer.

I've worked on a lot of different games, though all with an emphasis on narrative in some way. I started out as a games artist then became a producer for a while, but the majority of my work has involved writing in various forms and I even wrote a book called Writing for Video Games (although the book you're holding is much more hands-on).

But while I have a fair amount of knowledge and experience, I feel that I'm always learning, too. And I love the fact that there is always something new to learn.

A few years ago I created a game called Mr. Smoozles Goes Nutso, which I put together in a little tool called Game Maker. Even though I'd been working in games for about fifteen years at this point, I still learned so much in the process of making the game.

Creating any kind of game on your own can be challenging but don't be put off by this. Many popular games were created by people working in their bedrooms in the early days of the industry.

Today, it's still possible to do this – so many great tools are available that are either inexpensive or completely free. As you learn how to tell interactive stories you will overcome some initial challenges and gain confidence as you progress.

If you really love telling stories and like the idea of making them interactive in some way, this book will help you along that path. But only your own passion and dedication will take you all the way to your goal.

You can learn the skills you require and put in many hours to create excellent stories and games, but there are bound to be a few setbacks along the way that will test your resolve and dedication. Hopefully, this book will place you firmly on your path and give you enough initial insights to minimise the setbacks in the early stages of writing interactive stories.

Good luck and have fun!

ACTION ZERO

If you don't play games regularly or haven't played a game for a while, play some now.

Play games with a strong story.

Enjoy yourself.

If you're unsure what to play (perhaps your gaming knowledge isn't extensive) here is a list of some suggestions. You don't need to play all of them, of course, or indeed any of them. Or you can come up with your own list of games to play.

Thomas Was Alone

Broken Sword

Old Man's Journey

The Blackwell Legacy

Life is Strange

The Last of Us

Rhianna Ford and the Da Vinci Letter

Night in the Woods

Portal

The Wolf Among Us

Day of the Tentacle

There are tons of other games but if I listed them all it would take up the whole book.

Story Download

Because I use Twine extensively in this book, with examples of the things I discuss, I've made these Twine files available to download. You can study them and hopefully understand my explanations. The stories are numbered in the order I reference them in this book and I've placed these names in brackets where I do so.

The files are available here:

www.steve-ince.co.uk/ITGW/SI_Twine_Stories.zip

Chapter 2 – Storytelling and Interactivity

Games would not be games without interactivity. Game players blast enemy aliens, solve mysteries, race cars, and many other things, all of which require their input. Storytelling in games should involve some of that input; either the story itself being interactive or working with the interactive nature of the gameplay.

Game writers can draw on thousands of years of storytelling experience from other forms of writing, but also need to embrace new aspects that make interactive stories so unique, both in their creation and in the way they are experienced.

A Huge Industry

In my nearly three decades in the industry, games have gone from a small niche market to a huge industry now worth more than the film and TV industries combined. Games serve a huge audience where a large variety of people play, from young to old and across very diverse lifestyles. It's difficult not to find a game that might appeal to almost every person's interests in some way.

Game writing has developed into a vital part of our industry.

From serious stories reflecting the dark reality of human nature and history to dramatic, action-packed adventures to wacky comedic silliness to casual, time-filling puzzles, there are so many games that are fun to play. And a large majority also need the services of a game writer to help make the experience complete.

During my time in development and particularly the years spent as a writer, I've seen a lot of change, along with being fortunate to work on some great titles. Helping create games that people enjoy playing has been immensely rewarding and continues to be.

Here is a sample of the kind of thing I often write. Taken from the game, So Blonde, the main character, Sunny, approaches the main villain, a pirate called One-Eye.

Sunny:	I want a word about Diablo.
One-Eye:	Really?
Sunny:	He's nothing more than a big thug!
One-Eye:	That is the very reason I employ him. It's certainly not for his looks.
Sunny:	Well, one of you owes me the cost of a new cell phone after he smashed mine.
One-Eye:	I'll put it on my list.
Sunny:	You will? That's really good of you.
One-Eye:	My list of things to ignore.

Storytelling

Although writing dialogue is one of the best parts of game writing, there is so much more that goes into telling exciting and compelling stories.

We must come up with plenty of ideas, create characters to populate our stories, work out what our main character must do and how the antagonist will stand in his or her way. We need to make everything interesting, exciting, dramatic and funny, where appropriate.

Most importantly, it should be a story we really feel connected to and want to bring to life. For we all have stories we want to tell.

For instance, take my grandson, Louie. A few years ago when he was 6, I visited him when he was wearing a Captain America costume complete with shield. It was a great costume and he loved wearing it.

When I saw him again a few weeks later, he was wearing the same costume but his shield was missing. I asked him where it was so he rummaged in his toy box for a few moments before pulling out a small one belonging to an action figure.

When I remarked that it was a bit small, Louie quickly replied, "The bad guy shrinked it."

We all love making up stories and seem geared to do so from an early age.

Our writing is a great way to begin telling those stories. They might end up in a different form – a film or a comic book, maybe – but without writing down your ideas in some way they may be lost forever.

ACTION ONE

Our first proper workshop action is simply an exercise to get your brain warmed up.

Think of the kind of story you'd like to tell and write it down in a single sentence. Two at the most. It can be absolutely any kind of story you like.

If you need a little prompt with the type of story you might create, here are a few suggestions:

Swashbuckling pirate adventure

Space exploration

Teen romance

Problems at school

A mystery adventure

Police investigation

Ghosts and the supernatural

Climate change and the environment

Working with Friends

Creating story ideas and working them into more detailed stories can be great fun if you like to work on such things with friends. This can either be in person at home or in school or online through Zoom or something similar.

Many people prefer to work alone but others find working with friends fires up their imaginations even more. Neither way is preferable and it's really down to each person to work in the way that suits them best.

There can be both benefits and pitfalls when working with others.

On the plus side, things can move along faster when two or more of you come up with great ideas. You can also find ways to make a good idea even better when all of you have an input.

A little down side is that small disagreements about the simplest of things can side-track your intentions and waste a lot of time. So it's always best to keep this in mind and try to do your best to remain calm and focussed.

Working well with others is important when you get into a professional situation, but when you're trying to get to grips with some new ideas and ways of working, it can sometimes be better to work at your own pace. Think about which method might best suit the way you like to work.

Interactivity

Interactivity is the thing that makes game writing and storytelling so much different to writing for other media like films or books. It's this difference that makes it really exciting but also a little difficult at times.

This doesn't necessarily mean a game's story is interactive – some games have very simple stories – but the story must fit with the nature of a game's particular approach to interactivity.

Games have very different styles of gameplay and interactivity and even games within a particular style can vary a great deal from one another. We all love that variety in games. Game writers must therefore appreciate those differences and ensure the writing complements them for any particular project. But also, the approach to storytelling that works perfectly with one type of game may not work at all for another kind.

With such variety, a writer must be able to adapt from project to project and the writer's role may adjust accordingly. Generally speaking, the work is likely to involve, to varying degrees, story and character development, interactive plotting, scene development, dialogue and so forth.

Exactly how much detail goes into each part of this task list will be something the writer will discuss with the rest of the development team in general and the game designers in particular.

Game writers very rarely work alone on a project because there is so much involved, particularly on large projects. Those of us who work from home on a freelance basis still regularly Zoom, chat and e-mail with other people in the team, whether they are up the road in the nearest town or thousands of miles away in Russia, Australia or the USA.

Writing for games won't be everyone's plate of sprouts, but an awareness of what goes into game writing and an understanding of interactive storytelling may help you in your wider writing career.

There are an increasing number of interactive film projects and interactive theatre experiences taking place, along with games that use live action as an important part of the finished product. Even those

Choose Your Own Adventure story books are making a comeback.

Understanding how interactive stories and dialogue work within games can be a huge help if you become involved in any of those undertakings. And vice-versa, hopefully.

Play Games!

Game writers must play games and enjoy doing so.

In fact, all people who work in game development must play games. That may seem like an obvious thing to say, but I often meet people who don't play games yet think they have a great idea for a game. How can they know what a great idea for a game would be if they don't play them? Similarly, how can a writer become a game writer if they haven't experienced how story, characters, dialogue, etc. work in a game?

By playing games and researching various types of games, you can learn how players might think when playing those games and also that there isn't a one-game-fits-all when it comes to players. Players' tastes vary as much as the types of games they play.

Chapter 3 – Ideas and Structure

When it comes to writing, the first step is to come up with ideas, of course. Ideas are like exercise for the brain and without exercise it might shrivel and shrink.

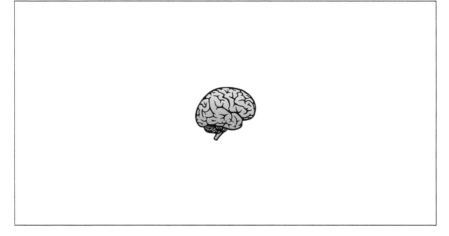

I think most of us could come up with hundreds of ideas a day, but sometimes we rack our brains and struggle to think of anything. The problem isn't having the ideas it's in *starting* to have them. Once they begin to flow your creative mind kicks into gear and it can be difficult to stop them. Though why you would want to do so is a little beyond me – there is nothing better than a mind full of ideas to think about.

But if you need a little boost, how might you start your creative juices flowing? Most writers have their own methods for this, which might include going for a walk or reading a newspaper, but I'm going to offer a different suggestion.

Rory's Story Cubes

The story cubes are just one means of generating ideas, but they can be a really useful process because of the way they introduce potential story elements in random combinations. You can buy them in sets of nine or download an app to your phone and they're a fun story game to play as well as a great way to spark story ideas.

If used as intended, you'd throw the nine dice and make up a story from all of the uppermost images. However, if you're using them as a catalyst to fire up your imagination, you can use them in any way you can think of. Whatever helps generate ideas and gets your creative mind in gear is perfectly fine.

So let's get your brains into a functioning mode.

ACTION TWO

Look at the picture of the cubes, choose any three of the images you can see and come up with a three line story based on them.

The three images you choose should represent the beginning, middle and end of your brief story. The story can be about anything and in any genre. It's your story.

You can be as open in your interpretation of the images as you wish. This isn't an exercise in restricting you but in giving you a starting point.

> At this stage, don't worry about exact spelling and grammar. You can always fix that later if you plan to show your story to others.

The Invitation

In case you're a little unsure of the kind of thing I mean by a three line story, here's a simple one I came up with to illustrate this, based on the same image of the cubes.

> One day, Gary received a strange invitation in the post.
>
> But the place on the invite was dark and the torch he always carried didn't have batteries.
>
> Then the lights went on and a round of applause rang out – it was a party for him.

Naturally, such a very brief tale gives little room for any deep story development. However, I can use this example to illustrate how there can be power in our use of words. Not only in what they say, but in what they don't say.

Because I've not described Gary in any detail, you'll form your own ideas about him – his looks and the kind of person he is, for instance. Your minds fill in the missing details.

Of course, I'm implying things in these words here. He's the kind of person who receives strange invitations. He has family and friends who like him enough to throw him a surprise party. And he's the sort of person who always carries a torch, even if he doesn't always renew the batteries.

And from the way I've written it, most of you are likely to assume that Gary is roughly the same age as you.

However, if I simply add one word to the last line:

> Then the lights went on and a round of applause rang out – it was a retirement party for him.

Now we have a very different spin on who Gary is. A young person doesn't have a retirement party, after all.

The choice of words can be really important to the story you want to tell.

Characters

Characters should be at the heart of our stories. It's difficult to imagine a story without characters, whether they are normal people, toys that come to life, magical creatures or invading aliens. Characters and what they do drive the story forward and need to be given some thought when writing your stories.

In my brief story about Gary, I didn't put a lot of work into how he might look as I wanted that to be filled in by the reader as I already mentioned. I wanted to use that to give two possible versions of him because of the way I used the story to make a point about words.

In most of the normal stories we write, we should have a clear idea who our characters are and why they feature strongly in the stories. What is in their natures that makes them want to save the world or solve a mystery? What do they do when confronted by danger or a huge obstacle? Are they good, bad or something in-between?

There are tons of questions you can ask about your characters but only you will know which ones are important. And you alone will know how to answer these questions.

ACTION THREE

Create a profile of a main character you want to include in your story.

Write a paragraph or two that helps you get to know who he, she or they actually is and how they might behave in your story world.

If it helps you to get a clearer idea of the nature of your character, create a rough drawing of them. Keep it simple.

Basic Structure

The reason I asked you to choose just three images from the dice earlier is because the beginning, middle and end of stories is something we often refer to as structure, at least at a very basic level.

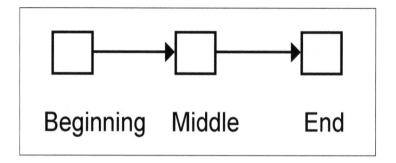

But the simple nature of a beginning, middle and end becomes much more complex with longer and richer stories. Films, novels and ongoing TV series have very intricate ways of telling stories, but they often have their starting point in the basic structure.

In games, though, it is even more complicated because of their interactive nature. For the moment, though, we'll stick to the basics and come back to that later.

Chapter 4 – Basics of Twine

Now we're going to learn the process of writing an interactive story using Twine, which you can either download to your computer or use directly online at **www.twinery.org**. Be sure to get the latest version if you download it.

It doesn't cost anything (unless you'd like to make a donation) and the file size is pretty small, so you won't fill up very much space on your hard drive.

Twine is not only relatively easy to get into, it also enables you to tell great interactive stories in the way that you want to do so. Once you have an initial understanding of the software you'll be sure to think of plenty of ways to tell stories.

When you first open Twine it will open on the Home Page and should look like the following image (though in colour, obviously).

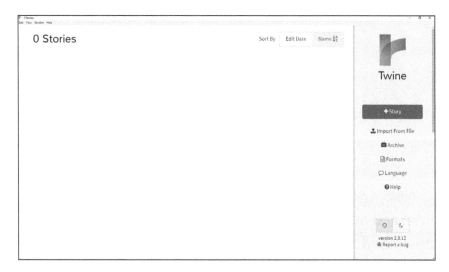

There are no stories because you haven't created any yet.

A friendly warning – do not use Twine with the Caps Lock on. This can cause problems with the way Twine works.

ACTION FOUR

Create your first story in Twine by following these steps.

Click on the add story button on the right of the window.

Give the new story any name you like and click on the +Add button.

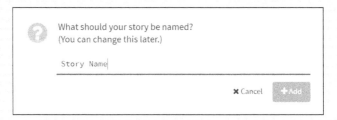

A grid now opens with an untitled passage.

You can position it wherever you like by dragging it around with the mouse.

Hover the mouse pointer over it then choose the pencil icon to edit it. The passage opens to show the following:

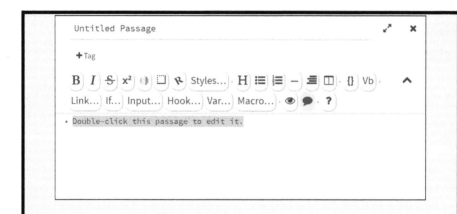

Close the tool bar with the arrow on the right (this cuts down on clutter for the time being) and it should now look like this:

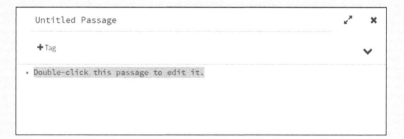

Give the passage a name by editing "Untitled Passage" at the top. It can be anything you want - Story Start, Chapter 1, Part One, etc.

Where it says "Double-click this passage to edit it." - if you delete this text you will see the following:

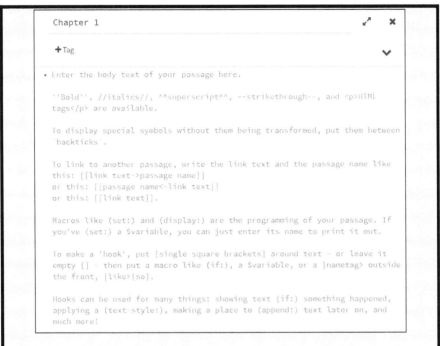

This is a convenient reminder of some of the formatting, but don't worry about this for the moment as I'll start to introduce these things as we go along.

Simply write some text in here to begin your story.

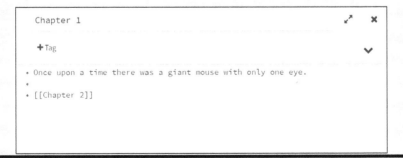

You'll see that I've put "Chapter 2" inside double square brackets like so: [[Chapter 2]]. This is how we create the links to other passages.

If you close this passage editing window you will see that a new passage has been created automatically with the name that I placed in the above link.

(See 00 Story Name)

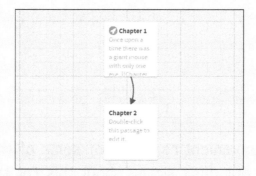

The passage will need to be edited to create more content, but you're already starting to create the first steps of an interactive story.

You can play what you've created by clicking on the "Play" button at the bottom of the screen. This will launch the story in your default browser for you to play through.

There is little in the story at the moment but I hope you can already see the huge potential.

The Hover Menu

When you hover the mouse pointer over a passage a menu of icons appears that allows you to do a number of things.

The bin icon deletes the passage, but it should only be used if you **really** wish to delete it permanently.

The pencil icon enables you to edit the passage.

The play icon enables you to play the game from this passage rather than playing from the beginning.

The icon with three dots will open another menu.

This gives you a number of further options.

The first enables you to set the current passage as the game/story starting point. The one in the image is already the starting point, which is why there is a tick beside the option. This starting point is also indicated next to the passage name by the little rocket in a circle.

The other options in the list allow you to change the shape and size of the passage as it appears on the grid screen. Small allows you to fit more passages onto the screen but you can choose other options as you wish.

Duplicating and Importing

If you want to keep an existing story unchanged but would like to use it as the basis of a new one, you can duplicate the story and edit that one instead. On the home page simply click on the small cog icon below the story and choose "Duplicate Story" from the drop-down menu. Then give the new story a different name and click on the "Duplicate" button.

You will also notice on the right of the home screen, just below +Story, a link that enables you to import stories from a file.

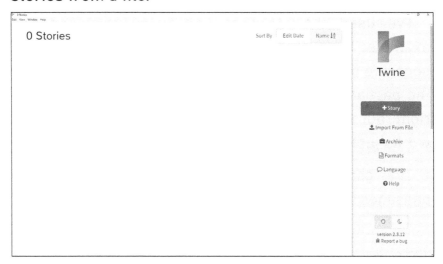

Stories are basically html files, so if you downloaded my stories earlier and extracted them from the zip file, you can import them here to study them and use them as reference. Choose "Import From File" and navigate to the folder into which you saved the stories.

Basic structure again

If we look at our basic structure again – the beginning, middle and end – we can easily create this structure in a Twine story. (See 01 The Invitation)

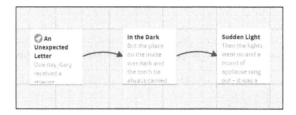

I've used the story of Gary's invitation for this example. I've placed each of the three lines in a separate passage and created the links. I've positioned the passages on the grid so the flow goes from left to right, but that's just my personal preference. Vertical works just as well if you prefer this.

The contents of the story are placed into the passages in the following manner.

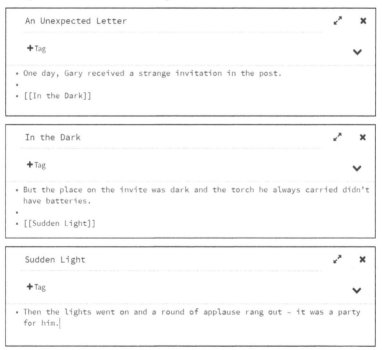

ACTION FIVE

Now, create a short, simple, three-part story in Twine that uses this linking. You can use your earlier story if you wish or create something new.

The amount of text you write for each part of the story is completely down to you but it might be best to keep it reasonably short at this stage.

Test your story by playing it using the play button at the bottom. Something this simple should work fine.

If it doesn't work, check your formatting. Make sure the double square brackets are used properly for links.

As I mentioned earlier, Caps Lock can cause problems so make sure this is off.

A Simple Game Narrative

Clearly, most stories consist of far more than three simple passages, game stories included.

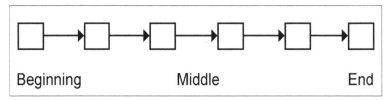

The longer our game takes to tell its story, the more story passages we would need to insert. Looked at this way, most games would consist of hundreds of these small story passages in order to tell us everything. But for now let's keep it simple.

ACTION SIX

Create a new story in Twine that's a little longer. Perhaps you could aim for about six passages.

Try to make the story as interesting as possible.

Again, check it plays through without any problems.

Setting up this longer structure in Twine works in the same way as before but with more passages linked together. (See 02 On Rails)

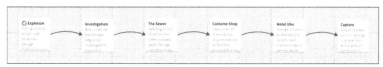

The example I've set up is a very simplified version of Broken Sword in which I've modified the early part of that game. Those of you who know the game will be able to tell how much I've simplified it.

Knowing this game is not required to understand the example, however.

As you can see from this image of the first passage, I've put more detail into this story, though the structure is still rather simple overall.

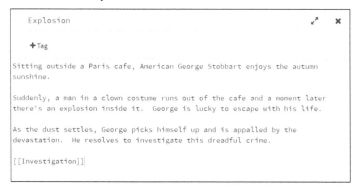

When a game and its story take on the very linear structure illustrated above, it is often referred to as being "on rails" because the player is unable to affect the story or stray from the gameplay path. There is nothing wrong with this approach if the game is fun to play and the story is exciting.

ACTION SEVEN

Expand your story so it has more detail.

Or if you prefer, write a new one that's a little more involved.

Think about what the extra detail can add to your story, but don't add in more words simply for the sake of it. Make it all count.

For those interested, here is the full text of my modified "Broken Sword" story.

Explosion

Sitting outside a Paris cafe, American George Stobbart enjoys the autumn sunshine.

Suddenly, a man in a clown costume runs out of the cafe and a moment later there's an explosion inside it. George is lucky to escape with his life.

As the dust settles, George picks himself up and is appalled by the devastation. He resolves to investigate this dreadful crime.

[[Investigation]]

Investigation

But no sooner has George begun his investigation than he is questioned by the police, though he is not arrested. The police tell him not to get involved but George wants to know who nearly killed him.

He quickly meets up with a young journalist, Nicole Collard, who suggests that this is simply the latest in a series of linked murders, although the police are denying it.

The two agree to work together and share any leads they uncover.

[[The Sewer]]

The Sewer

Heading in the direction the killer escaped leads George into the sewers. While they prove to be distinctly unpleasant, he discovers clues left by the killer.

George calls up Nicole to give her the news and she tells him that the clues point to a costume shop where the killer must have obtained his disguise.

[[Costume Shop]]

Costume Shop

The owner of the costume shop is evasive at first but eventually gives the name of the customer who bought the clown costume, along with some other disguises - Khan.

Using this name George is able to track him down to a small hotel called the Ubu.

[[Hotel Ubu]]

Hotel Ubu

George is forced to distract the hotel's desk clerk in order to get the key to Khan's room, but when he enters it he finds the killer is not there.

He decides to lie in wait for him.

[[Capture]]

Capture

When the killer returns, George surprises him and is able to capture him before Khan can resist.

With the killer secure, George calls Nicole to tell her the good news then makes a call to the police.

Investigation complete.

Although it's fun to write this kind of story, it's even greater fun to write stories with more interactivity.

Chapter 5 – Stories with Interactivity

When you look at the simple stories above and play them, the only kind of interaction is to click on the link that takes us to the next part of the story. Our stories can be so much richer than this and really deserve to reflect all of our cool ideas.

More complex interactivity is not a simple task so I will introduce it gradually, building up the details as we progress.

Structure and Interactivity

These two words might seem at odds with each other. After all, how can your story have structure if you allow it to be interactive?

Well, that depends on how we define structure and how rigid it needs to be when building detail. What structure means and how it evolves in an interactive story will soon be made clear.

Basic Structure 2

If we return to the idea of the very basic shape, not only will it fit the overall, larger structure, it can be applied to smaller parts that make up the whole.

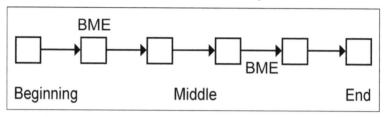

For instance, each chapter or level of gameplay will have a beginning, middle and end, created in such a way that the end of one leads into the beginning of the next.

Each small scene will have a beginning, middle and end, too. Our overall structure is made up of lots of smaller structures almost like building blocks.

This is where reducing structure back to a basic form makes a good point to start when applying it to an interactive narrative. The building blocks give us more flexibility.

Make a Choice – two doors

Making choices is important to interactivity, so imagine that you're playing a video game and you find there are two doors facing you, pretty indistinguishable from each other.

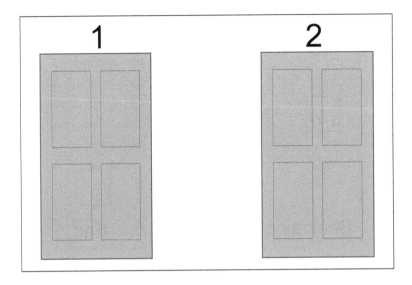

Which do you go through?

Make a choice – door 1 or door 2.

This is just a mental exercise, of course, but please remember your choice and I will tell you what happens soon. For the moment, let's look at how to give choice to the player in Twine.

Story Choices

If we look at another simple diagram, you can see that I've created a choice just before the end of the story/game.

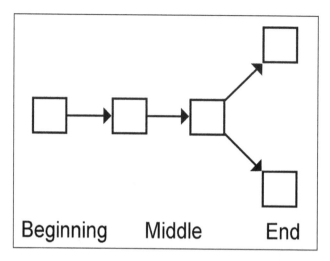

Beginning   Middle   End

In Twine I created a new version of Gary's invitation story to match this. (See 03 The Invitation 2)

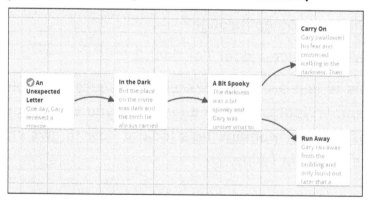

I added a new passage called "A Bit Spooky", which looks like this:

> The darkness was a bit spooky and
> Gary was unsure what to do.
>
> [[Carry On]]
>
> [[Run Away]]

As you can see, creating the two choice links is very simple – you just put a second link into the passage.

When the story is played, the two choices are shown on screen together and the player can choose one or the other.

The choices lead to the two endings below.

Carry On

Gary swallowed his fear and continued walking in the darkness.

Then the lights went on and a round of applause rang out — it was a party for him.

Run Away

Gary ran away from the building and only found out later that a party had been held for him.

ACTION EIGHT

Create a choice in your story so that there are two possible endings.

You can either use your existing story or start a new one from scratch. It doesn't have to be a detailed story as long as the choice is one that makes sense.

Play it and test that it works.

Types of Choice

Giving your player options to choose from sounds easy, but what kind of choice do you want to use? Here is a brief run-down of some possible types.

Moral Choice – These are the kind of choices where you are given the chance to do the right thing or not. For example, do you back up your friend when you know he's lying or do you tell the truth?

Action Choice – These are choices between different courses of action. Such as, do you try and jump on the departing train or leap in a car and try to get to the next station first?

Desire Choice – These are usually in the form of which things a person prefers. For instance, do you want lemon jelly or strawberry jelly?

Worth Choice – How much is something worth to you? For example, if you're trapped at the bottom of a well that's filling with water, which is the more valuable – a case full of money or a rope that will save your life?

Exploration Choice – These are choices that allow you to explore your environment. Left, right, north, south, open the door, climb the wall, etc. Making these choices will usually lead to new locations.

Investigation Choice – Choices of this nature are those relating to finding clues or information. Do you talk to one character before another or vice-versa? Do you threaten someone or try to persuade them?

Significant Choice – These are choices that have a long-term effect, perhaps through the whole of the game/story. For instance, if you break a family heirloom to get the key that's inside, your father may never speak to you again. If you find some other way to get it out the relationship remains good but you may have wasted precious time.

More Choices

We can, of course, expand on things and give more options for the player to choose from. Taking the modified "Broken Sword" game of earlier, I have added a number of options to the last-but-one passage. (See 04 Multiple Endings)

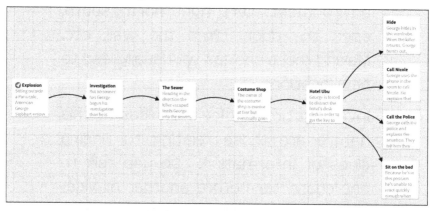

This works in exactly the same way as the previous example, just with more links created as shown below.

> George is forced to distract the hotel's desk clerk in order to get the key to Khan's room, but when he enters it he finds the killer is not there.
>
> There are a number of options now available.
>
> George can [[Hide]].
>
> He can [[Call Nicole]] on the phone.
>
> He can [[Call the Police]].
>
> He can [[Sit on the bed]] and wait.

What you will notice is that I have incorporated the links into sentences so the whole thing reads a little better.

The four outcomes can be seen here:

Hide

George hides in the wardrobe.

When the killer returns, George bursts out, surprises Khan and is able to capture him before he can resist.

With the killer secure, George calls Nicole to tell her the good news then makes a call to the police.

Investigation complete.

Call Nicole

George uses the phone in the room to call Nicole.

He explains that he's tracked down the killer to the Hotel Ubu and that his name is Khan.

Unfortunately, the killer overhears this from outside the room and makes his getaway.

George has failed to apprehend the killer.

Call the Police

George calls the police and explains the situation. They tell him they are on their way and tell him to get out of there.

He hears the killer at the door and climbs out of the window and onto a ledge where he is forced to wait until the police arrive and arrest Khan.

The killer is brought to justice.

Sit on the bed

Because he's in this position, he's unable to react quickly enough when Khan enters and, on seeing George, pulls out a gun.

The killer shoots him, gathers his belongings and leaves.

George has failed to trap the killer.

As you'll see, not all options are good options, but they make sense within the context of the story.

ACTION NINE

Create a choice at the end of your story with multiple options.

See how many you can invent without spoiling the story or creating too much disbelief in the player.

Once again, play and test.

Door Choice Outcomes

As I promised earlier, here are the outcomes based upon which of the doors you chose to go through.

> If you chose door 1 your character has just died.

> If you chose door 2 your character has lost all of their gold.

Unfair, right?

But that's how some games give choice to players – there's no way to know in advance or to work out what will happen until after you've made that choice.

You can only learn about the consequences of the choice by making it, which can be really annoying for the player, particularly if their character dies as a result.

It can sometimes feel that developers don't care about being fair to the player.

So games should always be created with the player in mind. Even if you're simply creating an interactive story with no other gameplay, you still need to take the reader into deep consideration.

In games, the player is instrumental in moving the gameplay and the story forward.

It could be argued that the "Sit on the bed" option in my previous example was unfair to the player as it resulted in the player character's death without fair warning.

However, George is in the room of a killer and sitting on the bed to wait is hardly the best idea. It's not unreasonable to hope that the player is able to work that out from the information available. Games aren't just about the obvious and often require the player to use their minds towards a little deduction.

By the way, if you didn't choose either of the doors earlier, that's perfectly all right. It shows that sometimes the choices in games are not always obvious. And from a developer's point of view, the nature of interactivity means you can't always be sure that the player will make choices in the way you expect.

Branching Narrative

If the player makes a major in-game decision earlier in the story it can affect the flow of the narrative and may well create a branch or branches in the story that will lead to one or more separate storylines.

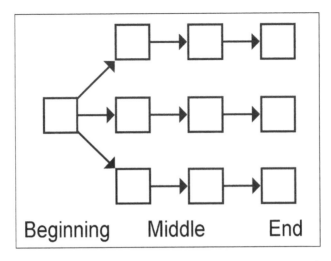

Beginning   Middle   End

For instance, you might have to choose between saving the dog or the baby or your best friend or your sister or the case full of money. Whichever you choose is likely to define how the rest of the story and game unfolds.

Also, whichever storyline plays out for you, the other possibilities are often closed off for the rest of the game so choosing carefully may be important.

In Twine, if we look at a branching narrative, we can again take the start of Broken Sword as an example. In the original game, after the explosion the player had a choice of things to do – go into the café, go down the alley after the killer or go up the street to see the workman. (See 05 Branching Narrative)

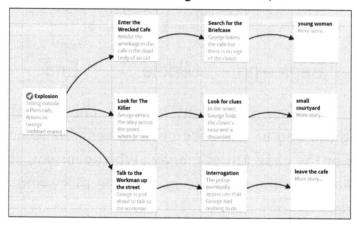

So rather than leave a choice until the end of the game, in order to affect the story in a bigger way, we bring it in much earlier – in this case, at the very start of the game. The first passage is only changed by the number of links we place in here.

Explosion

Sitting outside a Paris cafe, American George Stobbart enjoys the autumn sunshine.

Suddenly, a man in a clown costume runs out of the cafe and a moment later there's an explosion inside it. George is lucky to escape with his life.

As the dust settles, George picks
himself up and is appalled by the
devastation. He resolves to
investigate this dreadful crime.

He now has a number of options
available to him.

[[Enter the Wrecked Cafe]]

[[Look for The Killer]]

[[Talk to the Workman up the
street]]

The remainder of each storyline continues on in a linear fashion.

ACTION TEN

Now think about how you would create a choice at the beginning of your own story and how it would impact on the direction the narrative takes from that point.

It means you will have to set up an important story element from the very beginning or you will have nothing from which to branch.

If you want to keep things simple at first, try making the choice between just two options that branch into two parallel storylines.

Don't forget you can duplicate your story if you want to modify your existing one. Or begin again with something completely new.

Once you start working on it, how does this approach affect the way you view your story?

Do you see it differently?

Has the story changed its nature?

Change is a big part of the nature of interactive storytelling and it may make you think a little differently.

You will likely find that this is a big leap from the previous stories you've been creating. Suddenly you're effectively creating two or more complete stories that use the same starting point.

Creating parallel stories isn't the most ideal way of making a story more responsive, so how do we use interactivity more effectively?

Chapter 6 – Adding Complexity

In the previous story example, the branching narrative reduces the player choice to a single point in the game. The story could be so much more interesting and engaging if there were multiple points where the player could make a meaningful choice.

The danger with this is how do you stop it running out of control? By the time you get to the end of the game you could have hundreds of different endings.

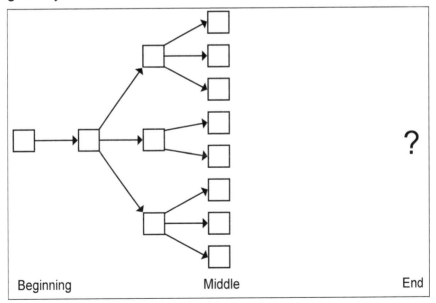

Beginning   Middle   End

Keeping Control

Many games give plenty of player agency, as it's often called, but still manage to keep the interactive story under control.

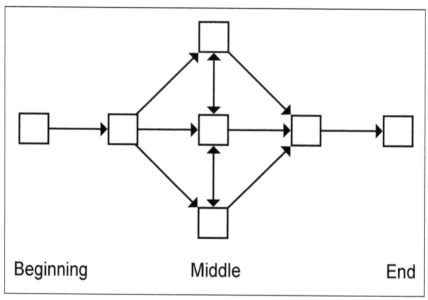

Beginning   Middle   End

Here, the choices link to a fixed number of story nodes with various connections between them. The player is therefore free to find their own path through the nodes using these links.

Even in this simple example there are nine different paths through the story. This means that, in theory, if nine people play this game each will experience the story in a subtly different way.

In Twine, I took Gary's invitation story and expanded it in a similar manner. It's not quite the same structure but you can see how it works. (See 06 The Invitation 3)

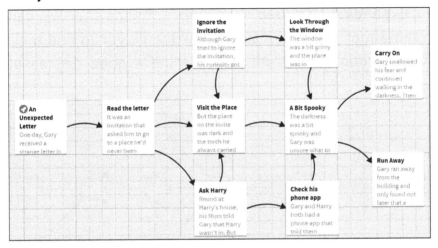

Sometimes we have to adapt the structure we aim for in order to better serve the story.

ACTION ELEVEN

Create a story that uses this kind of structure.

You may find that modifying an existing story becomes a little difficult with added complexity but feel free to do so if you are confident you can do it.

Otherwise, create a new story for this action point.

Again, take your time and try to plan it carefully. Test it as you go.

Adding More

Expanding this idea some more means that we can create more complex stories for the player to find their way through while still maintaining a good degree of control.

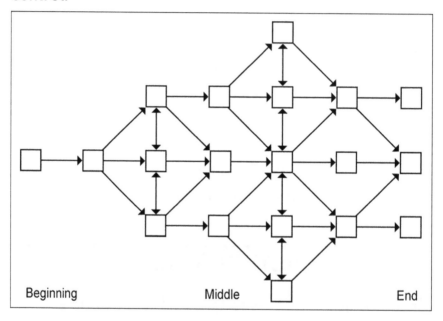

Beginning   Middle   End

Clearly, the more you add in terms of choices and paths, the more complex the story is to write. The image above looks so perfectly symmetrical and it's unlikely that any story would end up like this.

As you write something like this you may take out certain links because they're inappropriate or simply don't work. That's perfectly fine. The diagram isn't meant to be a blueprint for organising your story, just an illustration of the principles of offering choice at the same time as making sure the options don't run out of control.

Below is a more realistic example of how a much more complex structure may be created as the story and gameplay are developed.

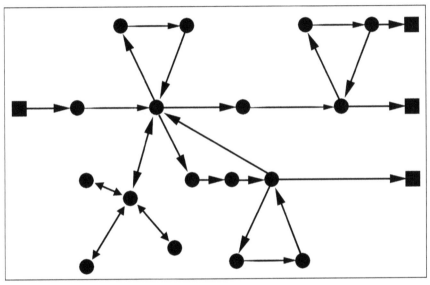

There are all kinds of paths through this story as well as places where the player must return to a kind of hub in order to move forward.

It's perfectly feasible to set up a situation where the player is given the same list of characters to save as earlier, but this time they might be able to save each of them in turn. The player could choose the order in which to save them.

This could still have an effect on the way the narrative moves forward – for instance, your sister could be really angry with you if you didn't save the baby first.

The choice at the beginning of Broken Sword didn't actually lead to parallel stories, but it changed the flavour of the beginning due to the choices the player initially made.

In Twine, if we look at this complex narrative example, this is a little closer to representing the start of Broken Sword as it actually was. (See 07 Complex Narrative)

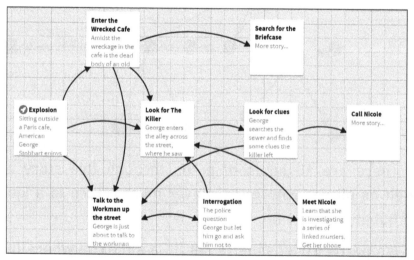

You can see that the flow gets very complex very quickly. Even if you don't use something like Twine to map it out, you usually need to develop flow charts in some other way to keep track of all the possible paths.

ACTION TWELVE

Add further complexity to your stories by cross-linking where you feel it will work. Don't force the links if they feel wrong.

Think about what this is doing to your story. Make adjustments as necessary.

Are you having trouble getting your head around this? Take your time and it will fall into place. (Not your head, the story complexity.)

This is what interactive plotting is all about – working out how to give the player the maximum amount of interactivity and freedom to explore without weakening the story.

Unfortunately, you are likely to come across problems very quickly and the example I set up has a number of issues which we need to be aware of and address if the story is going to work properly.

Chapter 7 – Problems and Fixes

My complex example has narrative loops, repetition and options that appear before they should. If you have downloaded my story examples, play this one and you will see what I mean.

These problems arise as a result of the narrative not responding fully to our actions. As players, we're making choices and reading each part of the story but nothing tells the system that this is happening.

In order to fix these problems we require some way of making a note of the things the player character has done and the information gained.

Boolean Variables

The best way to keep track of changes is to think in terms of true and false and use these values to switch on and off the things the player has seen or interacted with.

Boolean variables have exactly this quality – they can only ever be true or false. If used in the right way, such a variable can represent almost anything you want it to – yes/no, up/down, in/out, "I have an apple"/"I don't have an apple".

For those of you who think that we might be getting into the scary realm of programming, this really isn't the case. The use of Booleans really only comes in the form of checking values and acting upon them. It's about thinking logically and using the variables to make that logic work.

So if the player character learns the name of a cat is Milly we can set a variable to true. At another point we might want to check if this variable is true or false and if it is true then we could lure it over by calling its name. Otherwise, because we don't know the cat's name it will ignore us.

ACTION THIRTEEN

Think about your story and what sort of things might be represented by Boolean variables.

This can be anything but here are a few examples:

A light being on or off

The character knowing a specific bit of information or not.

They might have picked up an object or not.

You have the thief's address or you don't.

Booleans in Twine

Different systems have different conventions for the naming of variables. In Twine the names of variables always begin with the dollar sign. So a variable for knowing the cat's name could be:

```
$cat_name
```

Spaces are not allowed in variable names but you can use an underscore to make them more readable. However, this variable is not meant to represent the cat's name but whether the player character knows the name, so a better variable name would be:

```
$know_cat_name
```

By giving the variables understandable names you should always know what each of them represents.

Checking Booleans in Twine

In Twine, I've created a pretty simple story called Find a Clue. (See 08 Find a Clue 1)

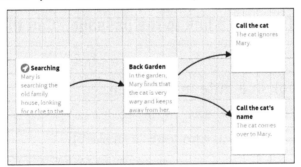

The first passage is fairly straightforward.

```
Mary is searching the old family
house, looking for a clue to the
whereabouts of her mother.

She spots a cat in the [[Back
Garden]].
```

But the second one, Back Garden, you'll find that I'm checking to see if the variable, $know_cat_name is true.

```
In the garden, Mary finds that the
cat is very wary and keeps away from
her.
(if: $know_cat_name is true)[
    [[Call the cat's name]]
]
(else:)[
    [[Call the cat]]
]
```

If it is true, I display a link to the passage, "Call the cat's name".

"else" means if the variable isn't true, so in this instance I display a link to the passage, "Call the cat".

If we look in a little more detail...

```
(if: $know_cat_name is true)[
    [[Call the cat's name]]
]
```

The condition statement in the round brackets, (if: $know_cat_name is true), must have the right format for it to be understood by the Twine system. The single square bracket following just after marks the start of what happens if the variable is true. The second single square bracket is the end of the instruction. It's important to get all these elements in the right places.

There is a chance of confusion here. Because Twine uses square brackets for two different uses, please remember that the double brackets create a link to another passage [[Call the cat's name]]. The single brackets contain the instruction based on the condition we use.

```
(condition)[
    ...instruction...
]
```

Written in plainer English, the above piece of script translates to:

If the variable, $know_cat_name, is true, place a link on screen that goes to the passage, Call the cat's name.

ACTION FOURTEEN

Create a very simple story similar to this and test for a variable in a like manner.

If you have any problems when you come to play it, check your formatting is correct.

If I play through "Find a Clue" I only ever reach the "Call the cat" passage because there is no place where I set the variable to true to trigger the other passage option.

Setting Booleans in Twine

In order to make this work I had to modify the story and add somewhere to set this variable (See 09 Find a Clue 2). It now looks like the following diagram:

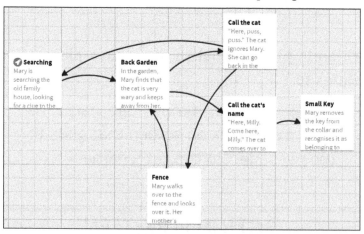

The passages "Searching" and "Back Garden" are the same as before, but I've modified "Call the cat". The player will now have two options in here.

```
"Here, puss, puss."

The cat ignores Mary.

She can go back in the house and
carry on [[Searching]] or she can
look over the [[Fence]].
```

Looking over the fence, Mary gets the name of the cat from the neighbour.

```
Mary walks over to the fence and
looks over it.  Her mother's
neighbour is doing some gardening so
Mary introduces herself and explains
that she's trying to find her
mother.

The neighbour says that she hasn't
seen her for over a week.

Mary asks if the woman knows the cat
and she thinks it's a stray called
Milly.

Mary can now return to the middle of
the [[Back Garden]].

(set: $know_cat_name to true)
```

I set the variable, $know_cat_name to true and give an option to return to the garden. Take note of the formatting for setting the variable – it will only work if this format is used (set: $know_cat_name to true).

So now if I play the story, the option changes in the passage, "Back Garden" after finding the cat's name so Mary can now call the cat's name.

```
"Here, Milly.  Come here, Milly."

The cat comes over to Mary and
nuzzles her hand.  On her collar is
a [[Small Key]].
```

As a result of this she gets the clue she was looking for – a small key.

```
Mary removes the key from the collar
and recognises it as belonging to
```

```
her mother.  Perhaps this is just
the clue she was looking for.
```

```
She just needs to find what it
fits...
```

The player has found their way through the story to the key Mary needs.

If we look again at the Back Garden passage we can see that both times we visit we will get the same text about Mary finding the cat very wary.

```
In the garden, Mary finds that the
cat is very wary and keeps away from
her.
(if: $know_cat_name is true)[
    [[Call the cat's name]]
]
(else:)[
    [[Call the cat]]
]
```

Using Variables for Variety

It would be better if we could improve the script so we don't get the repetition. In a new version of the story I modified the "Back Garden" passage so it looks like the following. (See 10 Find a Clue 3)

```
(if: $know_cat_name is true)[
    The cat is still wary so Mary
crouches down and offers her hand.
    [[Call the cat's name]]
```

```
]
(else:)[
     In the garden, Mary finds that
the cat is very wary and keeps away
from her.

     [[Call the cat]]

]
```

I'm checking the value of the variable in the same way but I'm placing more inside the instruction (or "hook" as Twine refers to it) – the two single square brackets.

What I've done is create two versions of the displayed text so that it reflects the changes that have happened based on what Mary has discovered.

The game will play in exactly the same way as before except that we get a different line of text when we return to the Back Garden.

Also, you should note that I'm now setting a new variable, $found_small_key to true in the last passage.

```
Mary removes the key from the collar
and recognises it as belonging to
her mother.  Perhaps this is just
the clue she was looking for.

She just needs to find what it
fits...

(set: $found_small_key to true)
```

I'm not actually using it in this short example, but if I were to expand this story it would be an important variable to check when Mary eventually discovers the object it's meant to fit.

Setting variables at key points – finding objects, obtaining information, etc. – is a good habit to get into, otherwise you will only have to return to that place and create the variable anyway if you plan to use it later in your story.

```
(set: $found_jam to true)
```

One thing you may notice is that the setting and checking of the variables happens invisibly to the player, but happens nonetheless. This is what we want, of course. If the player could see this kind of thing happening they'd be able to work out what was taking place. To the player/reader, our games and stories should appear to work seamlessly.

ACTION FIFTEEN

Now, you should attempt to use Boolean variables in a similar way in your own stories.

Perhaps it would be best to start a new story. Keep it simple at first and build on that.

Test what you're doing as you go by playing the game through.

If you have any problems, check your formatting is correct and that the spelling of your variables is consistent.

Even with the greatest experience, we all mis-spell the names of variables at times or put a bracket in the wrong place, which can be frustrating to track down. If in doubt, copy and paste your variable names and that way you ensure that they will be consistent.

Chapter 8 – Complexity and Variables

Good interactive stories are always going to have a certain degree of complexity to them and learning to handle that with proper planning and the careful use of variables will get you a long way.

However, if you feel that all these ideas have become a little overwhelming, take a step back, simplify your stories and keep them straightforward until you are able to get your head around these concepts.

You don't have to make things very complex in order to write good interactive stories, but it's worth taking some extra time to give yourself that additional level of skill.

Fixing the Complex Narrative

If we look at a new version of our complex narrative you can see that it looks a lot more intricate than it did previously, but it now works much better because of the Boolean variables I'm using. (See 11 Complex Narrative 2)

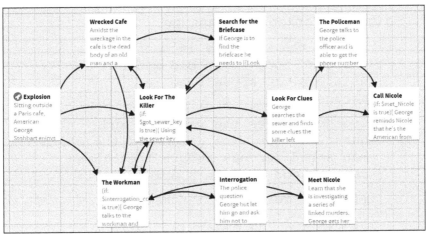

The first passage, Explosion, is exactly the same as it was in the previous version.

> Sitting outside a Paris cafe, American George Stobbart enjoys the autumn sunshine.
>
> Suddenly, a man in a clown costume runs out of the cafe and a moment later there's an explosion inside

it. George is lucky to escape with his life.

As the dust settles, George picks himself up and is appalled by the devastation. He resolves to investigate this dreadful crime.

He now has a number of options available to him.

Enter the [[Wrecked Cafe]]

[[Look For The Killer]]

Talk to [[The Workman]] up the street.

So is the Wrecked Café passage.

Amidst the wreckage in the cafe is the dead body of an old man and a waitress who appears to be unconscious.

George revives the waitress and questions her. He discovers the old man acted nervous before the clown came in and stole his briefcase.

[[Search for the Briefcase]]

[[Look For The Killer]]

[[The Workman]]

Search for the Briefcase is also unchanged.

If George is to find the briefcase he needs to [[Look For The Killer]].

He can also talk to [[The Workman]].

The Look For The Killer passage is a bit of a hub with lots of other passages pointing back to it. In this passage I test for a couple of variables.

```
(if: $got_sewer_key is true)[

Using the sewer key to lift the
cover, George descends into the
darkness with some trepidation.

[[Look For Clues]]

]

(else:)[

George enters the alley across the
street, where he saw the clown flee
to, and quickly works out that the
killer must have escaped through the
sewers.

Unfortunately, he can't lift the
manhole cover without the right
tool.

Talk to [[The Workman]].

   (if: $interrogation_complete is
not true)[

   Enter the [[Wrecked Cafe]]

   ]

]
```

The Workman passage contains a test for the
$interrogation_complete variable and sets another
variable, $got_sewer_key to true, which relates to the
previous passage.

```
(if: $interrogation_complete is
true)[

George talks to the workman and
manages to distract him.  He is now
able to borrow the man's sewer key.

[[Look For The Killer]]
```

```
    (if: $got_Nicole_number is not
true)[

    [[Meet Nicole]]

    ]
(set: $got_sewer_key to true)

]
(else:)[

George is just about to talk to the
workman and ask if he saw anything
when the police show up.

The detective in charge, Rosso,
takes George back to the cafe for
questioning.

[[Interrogation]]

]
```

In Interrogation, I don't check for any variables but I set $interrogation_complete to true.

```
The police question George but let
him go and ask him not to interfere.

Talk to [[The Workman]]

[[Look For The Killer]]

[[Meet Nicole]]

(set: $interrogation_complete to
true)
```

In Meet Nicole I don't check any variables but set $got_Nicole_number to true as well as a second variable, $met_Nicole. At first glance, setting two variables may seem a little unnecessary but the reason will become clear shortly.

Learn that she is investigating a
series of linked murders.

George gets her phone number and she
then leaves the scene.

[[Look For The Killer]]

(set: $got_Nicole_number to true)

(set: $met_Nicole to true)

In **Look For Clues**, I check if $got_Nicole_number is true. If it is George can call Nicole. If not, he can talk to the policeman.

George searches the sewer and finds
some clues the killer left behind.

(if: $got_Nicole_number is true)[

George decides to [[Call Nicole]]
and tell her what he's discovered.

]

(else:)[

George can talk to [[The Policeman]]
standing guard outside the cafe.

]

In **The Policeman** passage, George gets Nicole's number off the officer and is now able to call her.

George talks to the police officer
and is able to get the phone number
of the woman he saw taking photos
earlier.

He can now [[Call Nicole]].

(set: $got_Nicole_number to true)

In the final passage I check for the $met_Nicole variable because I want the phone conversation to start differently depending on whether George already met her or not. This is why I needed to have two variables because they serve different purposes.

```
(if: $met_Nicole is true)[

George reminds Nicole that he's the
American from the bombed cafe and
tells her about the clues he found.

]

(else:)[

George introduces himself and
explains that he was outside the
cafe when the bomb went off. Nicole
is cautious so George explains about
the clues he's found.

]

Nicole is impressed with George's
detective work. She invites him
over so they can discuss the case
further.
```

ACTION SIXTEEN

Examine the above logic and follow the links through in your mind. Take it slowly and think carefully.

You should be able to see how it all fits together.

Checking for Not True

One thing you should take note of is that in "Look For The Killer" I check for a variable being not true.

```
(if: $interrogation_complete is not
true)
```

In Twine, if I check for a variable being false it doesn't work unless I have previously set that variable to false. In order to check for variables being false in the story, I would have to set all of them to false at the beginning of the game.

This would probably be a good idea to give a sense of completeness, but it means that every time I create a new variable I would have to open the first passage and set the variable to false, which would be time-consuming and ultimately unnecessary.

So the best way to approach this is to check if it's not true.

This is why I generally check for variables being true and use else for the alternative (which is the same as not true in this case).

ACTION SEVENTEEN

With all this in mind, slowly try to expand the range of your own stories.

Create more variables and control the flow of the story by checking if they have been set.

Be very mindful of potential problems and test things as you go.

Chapter 9 – Scene Writing

Now I'd like to look in a bit more detail at writing a game's scenes. However, because games are very different from each other and have varying writing needs, I can't give you one single way to do this or a specific format in which to write scripts or dialogue for games.

I can only give you some idea of what to expect and the kind of things to think about when approaching the writing. Sometimes a game studio will be open to working with your approach but usually they have their own ways of doing things.

Above all else, you must be able to adapt to the needs of the project but the basic principles I'm covering should still apply.

Of course, if you simply want to write your own stories, rather than working for a studio, you can take all this on board and adapt it as you see fit.

The Crime Scene 1

In Twine I've created an initial sequence based on a crime scene. I've taken a number of liberties for simplicity's sake and I have only two passages. (See 12 The Crime Scene 1)

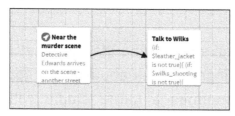

In the first I am simply setting the scene – Detective Edwards arrives at the scene of a murder and spots a guy called Wilks. The player is given the option to talk to Wilks.

```
Detective Edwards arrives on the
scene - another street murder,
another female victim, another
wasted life.

He takes a moment to gather his
thoughts then spots a guy called
Wilks standing nearby.

[[Talk to Wilks]]
```

The second passage contains the scene proper and looks quite complex. In here I'm checking a number of variables and setting a couple to true at the relevant points.

```
(if: $leather_jacket is not true)[

    (if: $wilks_shooting is not
true)[

        Edwards asks Wilks if he
saw the shooting but he says he
didn't.

        (set: $wilks_shooting to
true)

    ]

    (else:)[

        Wilks has nothing further
to say.

    ]

    (if: $johnny_shooting is true)[

        Edwards says that Johnny
saw Wilks near the body.

        Wilks is worried he'll get
the blame.

        He says he saw a man in a
leather jacket run away.

        (set: $leather_jacket to
true)

    ]

]

(else:)[

    Wilks tells Edwards to get
lost.

]
```

The `$leather_jacket` variable represents a clue and is only set when Edwards gets the relevant information from Wilks.

`$wilks_shooting` represents whether Edwards has spoken to Wilks about the shooting. If he hasn't (the first time he talks to him) we get the line that begins "Edwards asks Wilks..." I then immediately set the variable to true so we never get this line again. Preventing lines like this from repeating creates more believable conversations.

`$johnny_shooting` represents Edwards having talked to someone else called Johnny about the shooting. This part of the conversation will only be displayed once the variable has been set to true.

You'll immediately see that within the first if statement hook there are two others nested inside. This is perfectly fine and allows you to refine the logic when there is more than one thing you want to check for.

Keeping track of which square brackets are paired together can be fiddly but Twine helps in this respect. If you place the mouse cursor just inside the close bracket "] " the contents of that hook are underlined, which enables you to track it back to its partner bracket.

```
Talk to Wilks                                         ⤢   ✖

 ╋ Tag

(if: $leather_jacket is not true)[
    (if: $wilks_shooting is not true)[
        Edwards asks Wilks if he saw the shooting but he says he didn't.
        (set: $wilks_shooting to true)
    ]
    (else:)[
        Wilks has nothing further to say.
    ]
    (if: $johnny_shooting is true)[
        Edwards says that Johnny saw Wilks near the body.
        Wilks is worried he'll get the blame.
        He says he saw a man in a leather jacket run away.
        (set: $leather_jacket to true)
    ]
]
(else:)[
    Wilks tells Edwards to get lost.
]
```

There are lots of helpful things like this in Twine.

ACTION EIGHTEEN

Write your own scene using this conversational approach.

Think about what your variables represent and when you should be triggering them.

Think about what one character is trying to find from the others.

If I play through the above game I will only get the first part of the conversation. There is nowhere in these two passages where I set $johnny_shooting to true.

What's missing is a part of this sequence I haven't created here – a conversation with Johnny.

In terms of our simple structure, we have the beginning and the end in this passage, but because there is no middle, when we play it we don't trigger the end.

The Crime Scene 2

In this example I've modified the original scene so that it includes a conversation with Johnny. (See 13 The Crime Scene 2A)

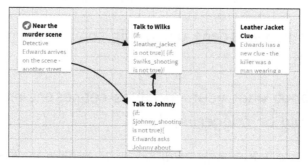

If we look at the Talk to Wilks passage we had before, it's basically the same but I've added two options at the bottom based on whether the $leather_jacket variable has been set or not.

```
(if: $leather_jacket is not true)[

    (if: $wilks_shooting is not
true)[

        Edwards asks Wilks if he
saw the shooting but he says he
didn't.

        (set: $wilks_shooting to
true)

    ]

    (else:)[

        Wilks has nothing further
to say.

    ]

    (if: $johnny_shooting is true)[

        Edwards says that Johnny
saw Wilks near the body.

        Wilks is worried he'll get
the blame.

        He says he saw a man in a
leather jacket run away.

        (set: $leather_jacket to
true)

    ]

]
(else:)[

    Wilks tells Edwards to get
lost.

]
(if: $leather_jacket is true)[

    [[Leather Jacket Clue]]

]
```

```
(else:)[
    [[Talk to Johnny]]
]
```

If we look at the Talk to Johnny passage, we can see that the guy tells Edwards that he saw Wilks near the body just after the shot was fired. I set the $johnny_shooting variable to true and give the option to talk to Wilks again.

```
(if: $johnny_shooting is not true)[
    Edwards asks Johnny about the
shooting.
    Johnny heard the shot and when
he turned the corner Wilks was near
the body.
    (set: $johnny_shooting to true)
]
(else:)[
    Johnny has nothing more to say.
]
[[Talk to Wilks]]
```

If I were to play the game, Edwards can talk to Wilks as before but now he can talk to Johnny, too. That sets the $johnny_shooting variable to true. If he then talks to Wilks again we get the information about the killer wearing a leather jacket.

Again, if we think about beginnings, middles and ends, we get the beginning, the first part of the Wilks conversation then we talk to Johnny to get the middle. Finally we talk to Wilks again to get the end of this little sequence and obtain the clue.

But what happens if we talk to Johnny first?

Talking to Johnny first makes the conversation with him the beginning. The middle and end are now in the conversation with Wilks. What this means is that the interactive sequence works both ways due to the way I set and check for the variables and the way I've written the conversations.

ACTION NINETEEN

Write a sequence similar to the above that has a beginning, middle and end, but one where the middle is in another place.

Make sure it works if you interact in a different order.

ACTION TWENTY

Write another sequence using conversations with three non-player characters.

> Can you still get the beginning middle and end to work? Do you need to change anything to do so?
>
> Do they always need to appear in the right order?

This Crime Scene story has been written in a very basic way with few interesting details. We can put in more detail as required in a style of our choosing. Here is a version with more story-like details. (See 14 The Crime Scene 2B)

```
Talk to Wilks

"Hey, Wilks."

(if: $leather_jacket is not true)[

        (if: $wilks_shooting is not
true)[

        Edwards greets Wilks like
an old adversary.  Their paths have
crossed on numerous occasions - none
of them good.

        Wilks is wary.  He's never
happy talking to a cop.

        "I heard that you
witnessed the shooting," Edwards
says.  "Just tell me what happened."

        "Get lost!" Wilks replies.
"I didn't see nothing!"

        (set: $wilks_shooting to
true)

    ]

    (else:)[
```

"I got nothing to say,"
Wilks replies.

```
        ]

    (if: $johnny_shooting is true)[
```

"Your friend Johnny saw
you with the body," Edwards says and
watches Wilks's reaction.

"That junkie ain't
fingering me!"

Edwards shakes his head.
"It's not looking good, man."

"Look," Wilks says then
pauses. "All I saw was a guy in a
leather jacket running away. The
woman was already dead."

"Thanks." Edwards makes a
note in his book.

```
        (set: $leather_jacket to
true)

    ]

]
(else:)[
```

"Get lost, will you?" Wilks glowers
at the detective.

```
]
(if: $leather_jacket is true)[

    [[Leather Jacket Clue]]

]
(else:)[

    [[Talk to Johnny]]

]
```

97

Talk to Johnny

"Hi, Johnny," Edwards says, approaching Johnny.

(if: $johnny_shooting is not true)[

"What can you tell me about the shooting?" he asks.

Johnny is wary. "What makes you think I know anything?"

"You always know," Edwards replies. "Whether you're involved or not."

"I heard the shot, but when I came round the corner she was already dead." Johnny is a little uncertain but continues. "But Wilks was near the body."

(set: $johnny_shooting to true)

]

(else:)[

"I got nothing more to say."

]

[[Talk to Wilks]]

The next version uses lines that are written in a more script-like manner. This is a useful style if the game you're writing for will have the dialogue recorded by actors. (See 15 The Crime Scene 2C)

Talk to Wilks

Edwards: Hey, Wilks.

(if: $leather_jacket is not true)[

    (if: $wilks_shooting is not true)[

        Wilks: What's up?

        Edwards: I heard that you witnessed the shooting.

        Wilks: That so?

        Edwards: Just tell me what happened!

        Wilks: Get lost! I didn't see nothing!

        (set: $wilks_shooting to true)

    ]

    (else:)[

        Wilks: I got nothing to say.

    ]

    (if: $johnny_shooting is true)[

        Edwards: Your friend Johnny saw you with the body.

        Wilks: That junkie ain't fingering me!

        Edwards: It's not looking good, man.

        Wilks: Look, all I saw was a guy in a leather jacket running away. The woman was already dead.

        Edwards: Thanks.

```
        (set: $leather_jacket to
true)
    ]
]
(else:)[
    Wilks:      Get lost, will you?
]
(if: $leather_jacket is true)[
    [[Leather Jacket Clue]]
]
(else:)[
    [[Talk to Johnny]]
]
```

Talk to Johnny

Edwards: Hi, Johnny.

```
(if: $johnny_shooting is not true)[
```

Johnny: You always turn up when there's trouble, Edwards. I ain't done nothing.

Edwards: What can you tell me about the shooting?

Johnny: What makes you think I know anything?

Edwards: You always know, whether you're involved or not.

Johnny: I heard the shot, but when I came round the corner she was already dead and Wilks was near the body.

```
    (set: $johnny_shooting to true)
```

```
]
(else:)[
     Johnny:     I got nothing more
to say.
]


[[Talk to Wilks]]
```

In many ways it's a good idea to keep everything as simple as possible until you're sure all the interactions and logic work the way they should. Then you can put in the details as you see fit.

ACTION TWENTY-ONE

Try writing your stories with different levels of detail or in a different style.

Develop your own stories into something rich and exciting, giving the player interesting options. Take it slowly and think everything through.

If something isn't working, take the time to figure it out.

Remember, you can duplicate your story if you don't want to change the existing one.

Until you get a bit of experience under your belt, it can be easy to miss things and create problems you can't figure out how to fix. Even with experience these problems never go away entirely as I've discovered on many occasions.

Working with a friend and helping each other out can be a great benefit as a fresh pair of eyes on a problem can be really worthwhile.

Each of you could also play through the other person's story and offer constructive help and suggestions.

You could also point out to each other if there are issues with dead ends, repetitions or links not working.

Don't forget, this isn't a test and there are plenty of right approaches to making these stories. As long as you can create an interactive story and enjoy the process you have already achieved so much.

Chapter 10 - Over to You

I've now given you a lot to think about and enough information for you to be able to create your own interactive stories, if you're not already doing so.

Mostly I've kept the examples short and to the point in order to demonstrate the ideas and principles I wanted to cover. But you can create stories of any length – simply use all these ideas to expand your stories into however big they need to be.

Working on small portions of the story at a time can help you build it up. As can testing thoroughly with each new part you add.

If you eventually want to create a really big story it might well be worth doing some initial planning before starting out. Perhaps you can break it down into chapters or something similar – that way you will feel a sense of achievement whenever you complete a chapter.

You might also want to consider creating an episodic story, where each part is not too big but they add up to a larger story when read together. This is similar to the way TV series work, of course, so it's a tried and tested format.

More Actions

Here are some further suggestions for stories, in case your mind has suddenly gone blank. But don't feel you need to work on any of these if you're eager to press on with your own ideas.

Feel free to interpret them in any way you like or simply use them as a starting point to trigger your mind into action.

ACTION TWENTY-TWO

Write a story with a main character very different to you.

Perhaps you can choose a different gender or someone from another ethnic background.

The main character could even be of a very different age to you; a grandparent, for instance.

ACTION TWENTY-THREE

Write a story with no human characters.

Perhaps all the characters are hamsters or jellyfish or dinosaurs. Or anything else you might think of.

Maybe you could invent your own race of characters from scratch, along with the world they live in.

ACTION TWENTY-FOUR

Write a story about an alien visitor who sees very different colours to the ones we know.

How might you explain why sunsets are beautiful?

ACTION TWENTY-FIVE

Write a story set in a world where money doesn't exist.

How would people view the world?

ACTION TWENTY-SIX

Write a silly story about an impossible pet that does weird things according to its mood.

Can its owner keep control of it? Where has it come from and how does its owner keep it secret from friends and family?

How funny can you make it?

ACTION TWENTY-SEVEN

Write a story about the best or worst day possible.

Will you make it humorous or serious? How will the characters handle this important day?

ACTION TWENTY-EIGHT

Write a story about time travel.

How might your character use it to change something they hate? What if someone else tries to use it to do harm to your character?

I'm sure there are tons more ideas you can come up with after reading those starting suggestions.

Exporting Your Stories

When you're happy with your stories, you might want to share them with your friends or members of your family.

To export a story, simply open up the story then click on the arrow to the right of the story name at the bottom of the grid page. A menu will appear and you should choose "Publish to File".

You are now given an option to choose where to save your story file, which can be anywhere on your computer, of course. If you want to give the file a different name you can do so, too.

Then share the saved file with whoever you wish and they can open it in any popular web browser to read and interact with.

If the people you share your stories with enjoy them you may well have to write more, of course.

Chapter 11 – A Little More

Before I finish, I'd like to mention a few more things relating to game writing and the processes involved.

Because games have incredible variety, it's difficult to apply the same details to each project, so I will talk about this in a very general sense.

Iteration

A professional game story is generally huge and told over many hours of gameplay. So, to write and develop it properly, it must go through a number of versions, improving and adding details with each one.

This process is known as iteration, if you didn't already know, and is vital to ensuring the story fits the design as both are developed.

It's pretty much impossible to write a rich game story without this iterative approach.

As an example, we might take the brief story about Gary's invitation I mentioned earlier in the book and create additional details, characters and plot twists with each iteration. We'd expand on details of Gary's life, create obstacles to finding the location mentioned in the letter, introduce characters he must turn to for help and so forth.

Iteration Pyramid

The process of iteration can be thought of like a pyramid where you start at the top with an idea that's low in detail and each layer down is larger because it has more detail until you get down to the base, which is where everything should be complete.

The analogy does not relate to building a pyramid because then you'd start from the bottom and work your way up, so it's more one of discovery and exploration.

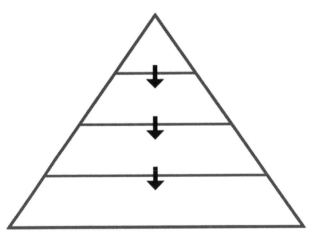

You might have a clear idea of the shape of the pyramid – the game story that want to create – but you have no idea what the details are that make up the insides.

So if you enter the pyramid at the top and explore one level at a time, as you finish each layer of detail – each iteration – you have a more complete picture. Until you finally reach the bottom and know the story inside and out.

In a very real sense, you're creating the interior of the pyramid as you explore the project's ideas.

Iteration Process

This is a very rough and simple version of the iterative process to show how it works.

High Level

The first layer of detail is probably going to be just a few pages of the main ideas and the main characters presented with the gameplay in mind to ensure everything sits within the scope of the project.

You should also create a brief story synopsis as part of this high level stage.

Story/Plot Outline

This is where it starts to feel more like a proper story with further characters added, the plot starting to take shape and where exciting conflict is developed.

Because the game is interactive and the story may have some branching aspects, it's usually a good idea to also develop a flow chart so you can see the shape of the interactive plot you're creating.

Level Breakdown

This layer is where you develop the story and design into a series of gameplay levels or chapters, depending on the nature of the game.

The story objectives and obstacles should tie in with those of the gameplay.

Each level may need its own flow chart and other diagrams, such as maps, but that probably won't be the writer's job.

Detail and Dialogue

Completing the story and design details is important before embarking on the final version of the dialogue. Only then will you know that everything is ready for those well-crafted lines the characters will speak.

Now, there are likely to be more stages than this, depending on how a team works, and each of these layers will likely have their own iterative process on a smaller scale as specific details are discussed, refined and agreed. Each could have its own iteration pyramid, so to speak. The number of iterations will likely be defined by how you and the team work together.

Dialogue

A writer is involved with many aspects of story, characters and so forth, but the dialogue is where the player gets the most direct connection to what they do.

Although the principles of creating strong dialogue are the same as in other media, the mechanics of how we go about delivering it can vary greatly because games are so different from one another.

It's important for a writer to be able to adapt to the needs of each particular project at the same time as writing great dialogue.

Some people have a natural flair for writing realistic dialogue while others have to learn this skill. Mostly it's about training your ear to listen to the way that conversations work. It's not just about what's being said but also about the way it's being spoken.

Script Format

Now, when writing for film and TV, there are script formats that have become industry standards in order to make things easier for everyone concerned.

With games, there is no standard format. Some think this is a bad thing but in many ways it's important for a script or writing format to be appropriate for the game you're working on. Game styles vary so much, so a format that works for an RPG probably won't work for a platform adventure.

Your Style

Of course, you don't need to write your own interactive stories in a script-like style. It's your story so you should write it in a way that sits best with your ideas.

You can use images or snippets of video. Create something that uses live action, perhaps.

Maybe you could just use recorded lines for people with sight problems, like a kind of interactive radio play.

You could write in prose or rap lyrics or even poetry.

For the game Godfire: Rise of Prometheus, I used a rhyming voice-over for the promotional video, which helped give it a grand, classical feel.

Writing and Design

It's important for a writer to work closely with the design team and these two aspects should really go hand in hand.

If the story and design don't link with each other the game can feel disjointed, so everyone must see the same vision for the game.

This makes it easier for the writer to create the various game scenes and ensure they match the way the design is developing.

It also makes sure that the writer doesn't put anything into the story that cannot be accommodated within the gameplay mechanics.

The Future is Exciting

Games and interactive stories can only get better as time passes. The tools to create them will improve, too. This is an exciting time to be starting out in this field and I hope you can build on the things I have covered in this workbook.

If you get to the point of creating quality, interactive stories, I hope you'll deliver all the excitement, conflict, drama, humour and character development you'd want to see in the games you play and stories you read.

Have fun!

Completed Stories

There will come a time when you have completed a number of stories in Twine and want to show them to the world. You'd probably love to show them to professional game developers and get their feedback. Please don't do this unless you're specifically asked to do so.

Most game developers are very friendly people and among the nicest you could hope to meet, but they are also very busy individuals. They would find it impossible to look at all the games and interactive stories people send their way. Not only is it a little unfair to ask them, you're unlikely to get the level of feedback you desire, which doesn't help you.

A better place to share your stories and get feedback is in suitable online communities, such as the one linked to from the Twine website, which has a variety of discussion areas:

www.intfiction.org/c/authoring/twine/46

There are plenty of other communities dedicated to interactive fiction and it's best if you do a search and find one that matches your interests. If you're young, you may need to get your parent's or guardian's permission to join these groups.

Above all, stay safe online.

Thank you.

Many thanks for reading this book. I hope it has given you a clear insight into how you can begin writing your own interactive stories and how this will help prepare you to write stories and dialogue for games.

ACTION TWENTY-NINE

Carry on writing interactive stories and those for games.

Don't be put off by any challenges — you can do great things if you are determined enough.

Appendix

Tools

This is not a complete list of game development tools by any means but it's a great selection to get you started. How you expand your knowledge beyond the scope of this book will be defined by the kinds of games you want to make and the way you want to make them.

Twine

After following this book you will already know Twine fairly well, but there is so much more to learn and explore once you get started. Well worth joining the community and looking for suitable tutorials that will help refine your interactive storytelling skills.

Inky

Another tool for writing interactive stories. Again this is open-source so it's free to download and use. There is an excellent tutorial that takes you through the basics.

www.inklestudios.com/ink/

Unity

If you're into more than the writing alone, this is a fantastic tool that has a free version you can learn and use. It's more complicated to use than Twine but there are many great online tutorials to help you. If you approach it in the right way you shouldn't have to do any programming.

https://unity.com/

I am currently using Unity, in combination with the Adventure Creator add-on, to develop my game, The Great Crow, which uses my Crow-Girl character.

www.crow-girl.com/crow-girl-the-great-crow/

Godot

This is another game engine and development tool. Free to download and use with plenty of instruction and tutorials. Like Unity, this is more suitable for those of you who want to go beyond writing interactive stories and get into game design.

www.godotengine.org/

GameMaker Studio

This is a game engine and development tool, too. Although you have to pay for this, you are able to download a trial version. There are plenty of tutorials to get you up and running and you can work in a way that minimises the amount of coding you have to do.

www.yoyogames.com/gamemaker

Some years ago I used an earlier version of GameMaker to create my game, Mr. Smoozles Goes Nutso, which can now be downloaded for free for the PC: www.juniper-games.com/smoozles/smoozles.htm

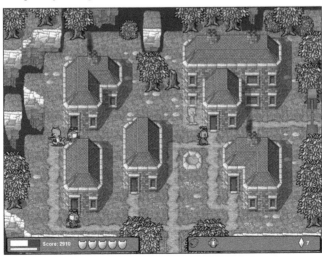

Eko Studio

I have only taken a brief look at this but it looks like a really useful tool if you're planning to create interactive video stories.

www.studio.eko.com/tool

Some Games on which Steve worked

Sword Legacy: Omen (2018)

The Bunker (2016/17)

Paranormal Society (2016 – 2019)

Broken Sword: The Serpent's Curse (2013)

Galaxy on Fire: Alliances (2013)

Special Enquiry Detail: Engaged to Kill (2012)

Captain Morgane and the Golden Turtle (2012)

The Witcher 2 – Assassins of Kings (2011)

Special Enquiry Detail: The Hand that Feeds (2010)

Rhianna Ford and the Da Vinci Letter (2010)

So Blonde (2008)

The Witcher (2007)

Mr. Smoozles Goes Nutso (2006)

Broken Sword – The Sleeping Dragon (2003)

In Cold Blood (2000)

Broken Sword – The Smoking Mirror (1997)

Broken Sword – The Shadow of the Templars (1996)

Beneath a Steel Sky (1994)

Talks and Workshops

Steve enjoys giving talks and running workshops, both online and in person and the book you're now reading is a result of gathering his workshop notes in printed form.

He has run sessions in various parts of the world from international festivals in Brazil to small groups in schools.

Should you wish to book a session or talk to Steve about the possibility of doing so, you can contact him through his website, www.steve-ince.co.uk

Other Books by Steve Ince

Non-fiction

Writing for Video Games

Fiction

The Quinton Quads and the Mystery of Malprentice Manor

Blood and Earth

Amanda Alexander and the Very Friendly Panda

A Few of Steve's Links

www.steve-ince.co.uk

www.gamewriterbites.wordpress.com

www.crow-girl.com

www.artstation.com/steve_ince

About the Author

Born and raised in Hull, Steve studied Astronomy and Astrophysics at Newcastle University before taking on jobs as varied as bingo hall management and metal refinery worker. At the age of thirty five he joined the games industry as an artist and has developed this creative career ever since, now working as a freelance writer, artist, designer and consultant.

During his eleven years with Revolution Software, Steve moved from artist to producer to writer-designer and it was in this last role that he gained a co-nomination for Excellence in Writing at the Game Developers Choice Awards 2004 for his work on *Broken Sword: The Sleeping Dragon*. The game was also awarded Game of the Year by *The Independent* newspaper and received three BAFTA nominations.

Steve turned freelance in 2004, concentrating on game writing and design, and has worked for a wide variety of international developers and publishers, including Wizarbox, EA, CD Projekt Red, G5, Floodlight Games and Fishlabs.

In 2006, Steve's book, *Writing for Video Games* was published by A&C Black and is still in print now.

Steve wrote and designed the adventure game, *So Blonde*, and in 2008 it brought him another award nomination; this time for Best Video Game Script at the Writers' Guild of Great Britain Awards.

Regularly invited to run game writing workshops and talk at numerous conferences and other events, both gaming-related and scriptwriting-related, Steve enjoys engaging with other writers and game developers. He is always on the lookout for new and exciting projects, too.

Steve recently held the post of the Videogames Chair of the Writers' Guild of Great Britain.

He continues writing for games, but in recent years has also penned two novels, a picture book and a number of screenplays. The short film, Payment, was made in 2016 by WriteDream Productions to some critical acclaim.

ACTION THIRTY

If you enjoyed this book and it helped you to write some great interactive stories, please consider leaving a review online and be sure to tell your friends, parents and teachers.